Aesop's Fables

THE
BANBURY CROSS
SERIES

Prepared for children by Grace Rhys

ÆSOP'S FABLES

ÆSOP'S · FABLES ·

ILLVSTRATED · BY · CHARLES ROBINSON

· LONDON ·

· PVBLISHED · BY ·

· J · M · DENT · & · C⁰

· AT ·

· ALDINE · HOVSE

· OVER · AGAINST ·

GREAT · EASTERN · ST · E · C

· MDCCCXCV ·

To Enid.

—ᴠᴠᴠᴠ—

ENID, this is Æsop's house,
    And the cover is the door;
When the rains of winter pour,
Then the Lion and the Mouse,
And the Frogs that asked a king,
And all the Beasts with curious features,
That talk just like us human creatures,
Open it, and ask you in!

G. R.

THE DAW
IN
BORROWED
FEATHERS

A CONCEITED jackdaw was vain enough to imagine that he wanted nothing but the coloured plumes to make him as beautiful a bird as the Peacock. Puffed up with this wise conceit, he dressed himself with a quantity of their finest feathers, and in this borrowed garb, leaving his old companions, tried to pass for a peacock; but he no sooner attempted to stray with these splendid birds, than an affected strut betrayed the sham. The offended peacocks fell upon him with their beaks, and soon stripped him of his finery. Having turned him again into a mere jackdaw, they drove him back to his brethren,

But they, remembering what airs he had once given himself, would not permit him to flock with them again, and treated him with well-deserved contempt.

THE SUN ·
· AND ·
· THE · WIND ·

A DISPUTE once arose between the
Sun and the Wind, which was the
stronger of the two, and they agreed
to count this as proof, that whichever
soonest made a traveller take off his
cloak, should be held the most powerful.
The wind began, and blew with all his
might and main a blast, cold and fierce
as a winter storm ; but the stronger he
blew, the closer the traveller wrapped
his cloak about him, and the tighter he
grasped it with his hands.   Then broke
out the sun: with his welcome beams
he chased away the vapour and the cold ;
the traveller felt the pleasant warmth,
and as the sun shone brighter and
brighter, he sat down, overcome by the
heat, and cast aside the cloak that all
the blustering rage of the wind could

not compel him to lay down. "Learn from this," said the sun to the wind, "that soft and gentle means will often bring about, what force and fury never can."

THE·DOG·IN·
·THE·MANGER·

A DOG made his bed in a manger, and lay snarling and growling to keep the horses from their provender. "See," said one of them, "what a miserable cur! who neither can eat corn himself, nor will allow those to eat it who can."

MERCURY.
AND
THE
WOODMAN.

A WOODMAN was felling a tree on the bank of a river; and by chance let his axe slip from his hand, which dropped into the water and immediately sank to the bottom. Being therefore in great distress, he sat down by the side of the stream and bewailed his loss. Upon this, Mercury, whose river it was, had compassion on him, and appearing before him asked the cause of his sorrow. On hearing it, he dived to the bottom of the river, and coming up again, showed the man a golden hatchet, and asked if that were his. He said that it was not. Then Mercury dived a second time, and brought up a silver one. The woodman refused it, saying again that this was not his. So he dived a third time, and brought up the very axe that had been lost.

" That is mine ! " said the Woodman, delighted to have his own again. Mercury was so pleased with his honesty that he made him a present of the other two, as a reward for his just dealing.

The man goes to his companions, and giving them an account of what had happened to him, one of them determined to try whether he might not have the like good fortune. So he went presently to the river's side and let his axe fall on purpose into the stream. Then he sat down on the bank and made a great show of weeping. Mercury appeared as before, and diving, brought up a golden axe. When he asked if that were the one that was lost, " Aye, surely ! " said the man, and snatched at it greedily. But

Mercury, to punish his impudence and lying, not only refused to give him that, but would not so much as let him have his own axe again.

THE·FOX· ·AND· ·THE· ·STORK·

A FOX one day invited a Stork to dinner, and being disposed to divert himself at the expense of his guest, provided nothing for dinner but some thin soup in a shallow dish. This the Fox lapped up very readily, while the Stork, unable to gain a mouthful with her long narrow bill, was as hungry at the end of dinner as when she began. The Fox, meanwhile, said he was very sorry to see her eat so sparingly, and hoped that the dish was seasoned to her mind. The Stork, seeing that she was played upon, took no notice of it, but pretended to enjoy herself extremely; and at parting begged the Fox to return the visit. So he agreed to dine with her the next day. He arrived in good time, and dinner was ordered forthwith; but when it was served up, he found to his dismay, that it was nothing but minced meat in a tall, narrow-necked jar. Down this the Stork easily thrust her long neck and bill, while the Fox had to content himself with licking the outside of the jar. "I am very glad," said the Stork, "that you seem to have so good an appetite; and I hope you will make as hearty a dinner at my table as I did the other day at yours." At this the Fox hung down his head and showed his teeth— "Nay, nay," said the Stork, "don't pretend to be out of humour about the matter; they that cannot take a jest should never make one."

ON a cold frosty day in winter, the Ants were dragging out some of the corn which they had laid up in summer-time, so as to air it. The Grasshopper, half-starved with hunger, begged the ants to give him a morsel of it to save his life. "Nay," said they, "but you should have worked in the summer, and you would not have wanted in winter."

"Well," says the Grasshopper, "but I was not idle either, for I sung out the whole season!" "Nay, then," said the Ants, "you'll do well to make a merry year of it, and dance in winter to the tune that you sung in summer."

THE LION · · · AND · THE MOUSE

A LION was sleeping in his lair, when a Mouse, not looking where he was going, ran over the mighty beast's nose and awakened him. The Lion clapped his paw on the frightened little creature, and was about to make an end of him in a moment, when the Mouse, in pitiable tone, begged him to spare one who had done him wrong without being aware. The Lion looking kindly on his little prisoner's fright, generously let him go. Now it happened, no long time after, that the Lion, while ranging the woods for his prey, fell into the toils of the hunters; and finding himself entangled without hope of escape, set up a roar that filled the whole forest with its echo. The Mouse, quickly recognising the Lion's voice, ran to the spot, and without more

ado set to work to nibble the knot in the cord that bound him, and in a short time, set him free ; thus showing him that kindness is seldom thrown away, and that there is no creature so much below another but that he may have it in his power to return a good deed.

THE CROW AND THE PITCHER

A CROW, ready to die with thirst, flew with joy to a Pitcher, which he saw at a distance. But when he came up to it, he found the water so low that with all his stooping and straining he was unable to reach it. Thereupon he tried to break the Pitcher; then to overturn it; but his strength was not sufficient to do either. At last, seeing some small pebbles lie near the place, he cast them one by one into the Pitcher; and thus, by degrees, raised the water up to the very brim, and quenched his thirst.

The Frog's
ASKING FOR A KING.

LONG ago, when the Frogs were all at liberty in the lakes, and had grown quite weary of following every one his own devices, they assembled one day together and with a great clamour petitioned Jupiter to let them have a king to keep them in better order and make them lead honester lives. Jupiter, knowing their foolishness, smiled at their request, and threw down a log into the lake, which by the huge splash and commotion it made, sent the whole nation of Frogs into the greatest terror and amazement. They rushed under the water and into the mud, and dared not come within a leap's-length of the spot where it lay. At length one Frog bolder than the rest ventured to pop his head above the water, and take a look at their new king from a

respectful distance. Presently when they saw the log lie stock-still, others began to swim up to it and around it, till by degrees growing bolder and bolder, they at last leaped upon it and treated it with the greatest contempt. Full of disgust for so tame a ruler, they carried a petition a second time to Jupiter for another and more active King. Upon which he sent them a stork, who had no sooner come among them, than he began laying hold of them, and devouring them one by one as fast as

he could, and it was in vain that they tried to escape him. Then they sent Mercury with a private message to Jupiter, begging him to take pity on them once more; but Jupiter replied that they were only suffering the punishment due to their folly, and that another time they would learn to let well alone, and not be dissatisfied with their natural state.

THE FOX AND THE GRAPES

A FOX, very hungry, chanced to come into a vineyard, where there hung many bunches of charming ripe grapes; but nailed up to a trellis so high, that he leaped till he quite tired himself without being able to reach one of them. At last, "Let who will take them!" says he; "they are but green and sour; so I'll even let them alone."

AS a Wolf was lapping at the head of a running brook, he spied a stray Lamb paddling, at some distance down the stream. Having made up his mind to make his dinner off her, he bethought himself how he might begin the quarrel. "Wretch," said he to her, "how dare you muddle the water that I am drinking?" "Indeed," said the Lamb humbly, "I do not see how I can disturb the water, since it runs from you to me, not from me to you." "Be that as it may," replied the Wolf, "it was but a year ago that you called me many ill names." "Oh, sir," said the Lamb trembling, "a year ago I was not born." "No matter, it was your father then, or some of your relations," and immediately seizing the innocent Lamb, he tore her to pieces.

THE · FOX · AND · THE · CROW

The Fox and the Crow.

A CROW had snatched a piece of cheese out of a cottage window, and flew up with it into a high tree, that she might eat it at her ease. A Fox having spied her came and sat underneath and began to pay the Crow compliments on her beauty. "Why," said he, "I never saw it before, but your feathers are of a more delicate white than any that ever I saw in my life! Ah! what a fine shape and graceful neck is there! And I have no doubt but you have a tolerable voice. If it is but as fine as your complexion, I do not know a bird that can match you."

The Crow, tickled with this very civil language, nestled and wriggled about, and hardly knew where she was. But thinking the Fox a little doubtful as to the quality of her voice, and having a mind to set him right in the matter, she began to sing, and in the same instant, down dropped the cheese; which the Fox presently chopped up, and then bade her remember that whatever he had said of her beauty, he had spoken nothing yet of her brains.

PRINTED BY

TURNBULL AND SPEARS

EDINBURGH

CPSIA information can be obtained
at www.ICGtesting.com
Printed in the USA
BVHW060747140820
586210BV00008B/351